DEEP DOWN
AND OTHER EXTREME PLACES TO LIVE

Written by
Shirin Yim Bridges

Cover images: Alamy Images: Mark Lloyd; Outdoor-Archive.

Acknowledgments: (Key: b-bottom; c-center; l-left; r-right; t-top) 123RF.com: George Burba, Mac Miller 8bl, 8br; Alamy Images: Anders Ryman 23t, ARCTIC IMAGES 22b, Ariadne Van Zandbergen 14-15t, 16t, 16-17, dave stamboulis 12c, 15br, Flonline digitale Bildagentur GmbH 24b, Horizons WWP 17cr, 17b, imageBROKER 16b, INTERFOTO 9t, Jose More / VWPics 10, Julie Quarry 7b, Mark Lloyd 6-7, National Geographic Image Collection 18cl, NPS Photo 10-11, 26, Outdoor-Archiv 18-19, 20-21b, Robert Harding Picture Library Ltd 12-13, 14-15b, Robert Matton AB 20-21t, stephen bond 8-9, SuperStock 11, tbkmedia.de 18br, 23b, The Africa Image Library 13t, Top-Pics TBK 21b, US Marines Photo 6b, 8l; Shutterstock.com: Aleksandra H. Kossowska 3tl, 14bl, dabldy 3bl, 4, Dr. Morley Read 3t, 5b, Fotomicar 25t, Isabella Pfenninger 3tr, 5t, MaxyM 24-25c, MrGarry 25c, Radu Bercan 25b, Tatiana Kholina 3r, 19b, V. Belov 3br, 22cr, 22-23.

ISBN-13: 978-0-328-83288-0
ISBN-10:   0-328-83288-X

15   22

DEEP DOWN
AND OTHER EXTREME PLACES TO LIVE

Written by
Shirin Yim Bridges

CONTENTS

Life on Earth

Most people on Earth live where it never gets very hot or very cold. More than half of all people in the world live in or near cities. More than half of all people in the world live within 100 miles of the sea.

Many of Earth's people live in quite similar places. When you watch a TV show, the places in which the characters live often don't look very different from where you might live.

But if you looked down at Earth from above, you wouldn't see many cities. A lot of Earth is jungle, mountains, deserts, or large areas of snow. What would it be like to live in some of these areas?

Let's meet some people living in extreme places.

Life at the Bottom of the Canyon

Deep down at the bottom of the Grand Canyon, there is a village called Supai. You can only get to it by foot, horse, mule, or helicopter. The people who live there call themselves the Havasupai. This means "the people of the blue-green water."

The blue-green water is the beautiful Havasu Creek that flows through the canyon. There are also four spectacular waterfalls that tumble down into the canyon. The water keeps the land around the village green. Many people call this place a paradise. But living in a place that is so hard to get to has its problems!

Grand Canyon

The Havasupai

CLAIM TO FAME:
The Havasupai are the people of the blue-green water.

HISTORY:
Havasupai have been living in the Grand Canyon for more than one thousand years!

INDUSTRIES:
Farming, hunting, and tourism

Supai Village

LOCATION:
On the Havasupai Reservation, near the southwest corner of the Grand Canyon National Park

POPULATION:
Around 450 tribal members

CLAIM TO FAME:
3,000 feet down at the bottom of the Canyon

CLOSEST NEIGHBORS:
Three to five hours away by foot, horse, or mule

VILLAGE

A Remote Paradise?

From the air, the Havasupai Creek looks like an emerald snake slithering between dry, red rock. In the past, the Havasupai farmed crops such as corn, squash, and fruit during the spring and summer. In fall and winter, the Havasupai moved higher up the canyon. They would hunt deer for food.

Supai Village

The Havasupai farmed crops like these.

DON'T TOUCH MY FRUIT!

Fruit trees were highly prized. They were such personal property that if someone died, his or her fruit trees were chopped down.

Farming today on the canyon floor.

As the tribe grew, the Havasupai began to run out of farmland. This was not the only problem. Sometimes the canyon would flood too, damaging crops. They needed to find a new way to survive at the bottom of the canyon.

The Blue-Green Water

Nowadays, the Havasupai make a living from tourism. The famous canyon attracts more than 20,000 visitors per year. Most visitors make the three-to-five-hour journey to Supai on horseback or mule. The Havasupai now run campgrounds, a café, a trading post, and a lodge.

YOU'VE GOT MAIL

Letters addressed to Supai are brought by mule train. It is the last U.S. Postal Service mule train left in the country!

THE FOUR FALLS

SUPAI FALLS:
Closest to the village

NAVAJO FALLS:
¼ mile beyond Supai Falls

HAVASU FALLS:
¾ mile beyond Navajo Falls

MOONEY FALLS:
I mile beyond Havasu Falls. It is the highest of the falls, at 190 feet high

Havasu Falls is the most photographed of the blue-green falls.

Surviving in One of Earth's Hottest Spots

In the middle of the Great Rift Valley in Ethiopia is the Danakil Depression. This region looks like a different planet. It is one of the hottest spots on Earth. It is heated from above by the sun and from below by lava flows.

You would think that nobody could live there, but it is home to the Afar. The Afar are nomadic people who come to the Danakil Depression every day to mine salt.

NOT A COOL BREEZE

Fire winds blow through the Danakil Depression. They are said to feel like a tornado in an oven!

The Danakil Depression

CLAIM TO FAME:
Daily temperatures of more than 120°F!

ALTITUDE:
300 feet below sea level

RAINFALL:
Less than 7 inches a year

CLOSEST CITY:
Mek'ele, 60 miles away

Danakil • Depression

Afar Gold

Ten thousand years ago, the Danakil Depression was part of the Red Sea. The waters have evaporated and left behind salt flats. To the Afar, this salt is like gold. Until recently, blocks of salt called *amolé* were used as money in Ethiopia. Today, northern Afar people still earn money from selling salt.

Camel Caravans

Every day, Afar miners come to the salt flats with around 2,000 camels and 1,000 donkeys. They transport amolé into the cities. The salt blocks are cut by hand. Everybody in the community takes part. The walk from town to the salt flats and back can take six days.

The Salt Trade

WEIGHT OF ONE SALT BLOCK, OR AMOLÉ: About 9 pounds

NUMBER OF BLOCKS PER CAMEL: 30

DISTANCE TRAVELED PER DAY: 15.5 MILES

The Afar live in huts called *aris*.

What Is Life Like in an Ari?

The Afar cross the Danakil Depression to mine salt. They then sell it in the cities. The Afar can do this because they bring their homes with them. They pack their houses, called *aris*, onto the backs of their camels. They usually put up their aris around wells. The aris are round, like igloos, and are made from light palm matting. They provide welcome shade in which to cook, eat, and sleep.

What's Cooking?

WHAT THE AFAR USUALLY EAT:
Meat

WHAT THEY EAT IT WITH:
Thick wheat pancakes

WHAT THE AFAR DRINK:
Milk

HOW THE AFAR SAY "WELCOME":
They give their guests a drink of milk!

HERDING ANIMALS

In addition to mining salt, most Afar herd sheep, goats, cattle, and camels.

Roaming the Arctic Circle

Arctic Circle

Sami homeland

Did you know there are people who use reindeer to pull their sleds? The Sami people do this. In the past, the Sami spent their lives roaming the Arctic. They followed the enormous reindeer herds.

The Sami Homeland

CLAIM TO FAME:
This is the farthest north that human beings live—200 miles north of the Arctic Circle!

AREA:
150,000 square miles, about the size of Norway

COUNTRIES:
Sápmi, the Sami name for this area, spreads across what is now northern Norway, Sweden, Finland, and Russia's Kola Peninsula.

UNDERNEATH THE MIDNIGHT SUN

The Sami live so far north that in the summer the sun never sets!

19

The Reindeer Walkers

The Sami call people who herd reindeer *boazovázzi*. This means "reindeer walkers." The herders used to follow the reindeer by foot or on skis. They now use snowmobiles to herd their reindeer.

An All-in-One Animal

Reindeer provide the Sami with meat, hides, and antlers. Most reindeer are allowed to roam free. Some are kept for milking and to pull sleds. Some reindeer can even be saddled like horses!

The Many Uses of Reindeer

FOOD: Reindeer meatballs, reindeer sausage, and smoked reindeer are all very popular.

MILK: Reindeer can be milked like cows.

MEDICINE: Reindeer antlers are sold to China because many Chinese people believe the antlers have medicinal properties.

CLOTHING: Reindeer have hairs that are hollow and filled with air. This trapped air makes reindeer fur very warm.

TRANSPORT: Reindeer can be trained to pull sleds; larger species can be ridden like horses.

TOOLS: Traditionally, reindeer bones were made into tools such as needles and knives.

That's Not a Tepee, That's a Lavut

When moving with their herds, the Sami still live in cone-shaped tents. These are called *lavuts*. A lavut can stand winds that are 50 miles an hour. The top of each lavut is open to let out the smoke from large fires.

WHY THE POINTY TOES?

The turned-up, pointy toes of a traditional Sami reindeer-skin boot are designed to hook onto skis.

Can I Please Take a Look at Your Gakti?

The lavut is not the only part of Sami life still in use today. The traditional Sami clothing is called the *gakti*. It is still often worn on special occasions. The colors, patterns, and buttons of a gakti are a code. They can tell you whether the person is married and which village he or she comes from.

ROUND OR SQUARE BUTTONS?

Traditionally, square buttons mean a person is married. Round buttons mean a person is not married.

23

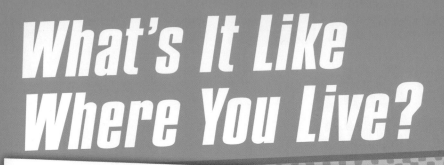

What's It Like Where You Live?

Now you've seen some of the extreme places where people live. What do you think might be extreme about your neighborhood? To an Afar child, where and how you live might look pretty different. Many people on this planet have never seen some of the things you probably see every day.

Imagine meeting someone from the Sami or Afar tribe. What would seem extreme to them about your normal life?

Glossary

lava flow   flowing or solid rock that erupted from a volcano

medicinal   having healing properties

nomadic   moving home from place to place

salt flat   area of flat land covered with a layer of salt

species   group of animals or plants that have similar features

Index

27